# CREATIVE CANDLE MAKING

12 Unique Projects to Make Candles for All Occasions

MEREDITH MENNITT

becker&mayer! books

Brimming with creative inspiration, how-to projects, and useful information to enrich your everyday life, Quarto Knows is a favorite destination for those pursuing their interests and passions. Visit our site and dig deeper with our books into your area of interest: Quarto Creates, Quarto Cooks, Quarto Homes, Quarto Lives, Quarto Drives, Quarto Explores, Quarto Gifts, or Quarto Kids.

Published in 2019 by becker&mayer! books, an imprint of The Quarto Group, 11120 NE 33rd Place, Suite 201, Bellevue, WA 98004 USA.
**www.QuartoKnows.com**

becker&mayer! books titles are also available at discount for retail, wholesale, promotional, and bulk purchase. For details, contact the Special Sales Manager by email at specialsales@quarto.com or by mail at The Quarto Group, Attn: Special Sales Manager, 100 Cummings Center, Suite 265D Beverly, MA 01915 USA.

19 20 21 22 23    5 4 3 2 1

ISBN: 978-0-7603-6615-8

Library of Congress Cataloging-in-Publication Data available upon request.

Author: Meredith Mennitt
Design: Kate Sinclair
Editorial: Meredith Mennitt
Production: Michael Nash
Photography: Chris Burrows

Printed, manufactured, and assembled in Shenzhen, China, 7/19

Distributed by:
Quarto UK, The Old Brewery
6 Blundell Street, London N7 9BH, UK
Allen & Unwin
30 Centre Rd, Scoresby VIC 3179, AUS

Image credits: All stock photographs and design elements © Shutterstock

328982

# CONTENTS

Introduction ....................................................4

What's Included in This Kit.........................5

Ingredients & Other Materials....................6

Tools of Candle Making ............................8

A Word on Wax ......................................9

Dos and Don'ts .....................................10

Troubleshooting ....................................11

## WINTER

Project 1: Candy Cane Candles ....................14

Project 2: Cookie Cutter Candles..................16

Project 3: Beeswax Forest Candles ...............18

## SPRING

Project 4: Lemon Beeswax Candles...............22

Project 5: Spring Fling Mason Jar Candles...............24

Project 6: Lots of Love Candles...................26

## SUMMER

Project 7: Summer Nights Floating Candles ............32

Project 8: Beach Bum Sand Candles........................34

Project 9: Modern Pillar Candles ...............36

## FALL

Project 10: Tea for Two Candles ...............42

Project 11: Coffee Date Candles ...............44

Project 12: Apple Cinnamon Votive Candles............46

# INTRODUCTION

Consider the candle: a household essential before electricity, a poet's metaphor for everything from desire to the divine, and an object used in every religion. There are few items that have influenced humanity more than the candle. Yet historians are relatively in the dark when it comes to its origin. Oil lamps are found as far back as 3000 BC, but it is the Romans who are credited with creating the first wicked candles. Wicked candles were safer, brighter, and cleaner burning than oil lamps, which tended to spill when carried.

By the Middle Ages, candle making had become an official guild craft in most of Europe. Within a span of a hundred years, the Industrial Revolution brought the mass production of candles, but it was quickly followed by the decline of the candle-making industry with the advent of electric lighting.

We don't need candles to light our homes today, and yet candles still have a hold on us. What would a romantic dinner be without candlelight? What is the coziest way to brighten a room on a winter night?

The only problem is that store-bought candles are expensive! Yet candle making requires very little equipment to get started, and the materials such as wax and scents are modestly priced. Some ingredients you might already have at home! So it's no wonder the craft of candle making has experienced a revival.

My goal is to get you started making some beautiful handmade candles. I hope this book informs and inspires you and that soon you'll be basking in the warm flicker of your own candles.

# WHAT'S INCLUDED IN THIS KIT

To get you started with candle making, the following materials are included with this kit. These materials can be used to make:

Project 3: Beeswax Forest Candles

Project 7: Summer Nights Floating Candles

**SHEET OF BEESWAX**

**7 oz. (200 g) OF SOY WAX FLAKES**

**FLOATING CANDLE MOLD**

**OSMANTHUS FLOWER FRAGRANCE**

**2 MOUNTED COTTON WICKS**

**12" (30 cm) OF WOVEN COTTON WICKING**

# INGREDIENTS & OTHER MATERIALS

Candles are all about customizing scents and ingredients to get different desired effects. Here are ingredients you may need to make the twelve projects in this book:

CINNAMON STICKS

BEESWAX

TEACUP

COOKIE CUTTERS

STIR STICKS / CHOPSTICKS

SMALL BOWLS

MASON JARS

COFFEE BEANS

CANDY MOLD

LOOSE LEAF TEA

DRIED ROSE
PETALS

LEMONS

STEMLESS WINE
GLASSES

WOODEN
WICKS

BERGAMOT
OIL

PEPPERMINT
OIL

BLACK PAINT

WAX DYE: RED, NEON PINK,
BRIGHT YELLOW, BROWN,
GREEN, BLUE TEAL

PLASTER

BOWL OF
SAND

# TOOLS OF CANDLE MAKING

There are two main tools that you need to invest in that will make candle making consistent, successful, and enjoyable.

## WAX POT AND WATER BATH

A metal pouring pitcher, which I affectionately refer to as "the wax pot," is probably the most essential tool in candle making. Invest in a metal pour pitcher (they're available online or in your local craft store for $10–$20) that you dedicate to the craft. It heats wax evenly and its spout makes pouring the wax much easier. Additionally, it is almost impossible to remove all of the wax residue once you melt wax in a pot, making it undesirable to cook in again. So save your cookware and get a wax pot.

It is important to heat wax slowly and evenly to avoid burning it. The easiest way to do this is to use a water bath or bain-marie. This sounds fancy but it is actually easy to do. To make a stovetop water bath, find a small cooking pot that your wax pitcher will fit inside. Make sure the pitcher touches the bottom. As you see in the photo, the walls of my cooking pot are low enough that the wax pitcher touches the bottom, while its Bakelite handle rests outside of the pot.

Once you find a perfect pot, fill it with two to three inches of water. Place the wax pitcher inside it and place both on your stove. Your wax will melt slowly and evenly.

## THERMOMETER

A candy thermometer is also a helpful tool in candle making. Not only can wax burn and discolor if it gets too hot, but it needs to cool to the right temperature to avoid creating cracks and sinkholes in your candle.

# A WORD ON WAX

## Paraffin Wax

Paraffin wax is the most commonly used wax in commercial candles due to its low cost. Paraffin is a byproduct of refining crude oil. It's white and odorless.

## Beeswax

Made by busy bees, beeswax is known for its soft honey color and aroma. Beeswax is more expensive than paraffin as it is less readily available, but it does burn cleaner and longer.

## Soy Wax

Soy wax is another natural alternative to paraffin. It is made from soybeans. It burns cleanly and up to 50 percent longer than paraffin candles. Soy wax can be easily dyed and scented. It is the primary wax used for most of the recipes in this book.

# DOS AND DON'TS

### DO read the instructions.

Read the instructions all the way through before you begin each project. Some steps are time sensitive and need to happen in rapid succession because we're dealing with quickly cooling wax.

### DON'T wait to clean up.

Once wax has cooled, it is a pain to scrape off. It is easiest to clean up wax while it is still liquid. When you are switching wax colors in a project, use a paper towel to wipe out your wax pot so you can start on a new color.

### DO prep for the mess.

Step one in candle making is accepting the fact that you are going to make a mess. Wax, dyes, fragrant oils; something will spill! So before you begin, cover your work area in newspaper or even a drop cloth.

### DON'T get impatient.

Candles don't take a lot of time to make, but it is necessary to wait eight to twelve hours (depending on the size of the candle) for your candle to fully cool and harden. Lighting your candle before it is fully hardened will significantly shorten the burn time of your candle.

### DO add your fragrance when the wax is at the proper temperature.

In order to get wax to be fully infused with your fragrance, it needs to be at a high temperature (180°F–185°F). Also, once you've added your fragrance, be sure to stir the wax for at least two to three minutes so the fragrance is thoroughly bonded to the wax.

### DON'T pour your leftover wax down the drain.

Waxy pipes will lead to plumbing headaches. Also don't put your wax pot in the dishwasher. Pour extra, unused wax in a paper towel or disposable container, allow to cool, and throw it in the trash.

# TROUBLESHOOTING

## SINKHOLES AND CRACKS!

These two words can strike fear into the hearts of any candle maker. You work so hard melting, mixing, and pouring then you return to your dried candle only to discover it's cracked, pocked, and, well . . . ugly.

Don't worry, it happens to the best of us, especially when creating soy wax container candles. Sinkholes and cracks occur when the hot liquid wax cools too rapidly and retracts, leaving empty spaces that did not appear when the wax was molten. Fortunately, it's a pretty easy fix: fill the visible sinkhole with more molten wax. And to prevent them from happening in the future, allow your molten wax to cool to a lower temperature (between 135°F–145°F) before pouring it into the container.

## JUMP LINES!

I just told you to let your wax cool way down before pouring it, but wax is a finicky mistress and occasionally, if you pour the wax in the container when it is too cool, jump lines can form. Jump lines are ragged, horizontal lines that appear on the sides of container candles and give them a rough appearance. They are purely an aesthetic problem and can be combated by warming up your glass container before you pour the wax into it.

# WINTER CANDLES

# CANDY CANE CANDLES

→→→→ ◆ ←←←←

Spread some holiday cheer with these
peppermint container candles.

## MATERIALS (Fig. A)

- 13 oz. (375 g) soy wax flakes
- (2) 8 oz. (250 ml) mason jars
- (2) 6" (15 cm) mounted cotton wicks
- 20 drops peppermint essential oil or candle scent
- Red wax color chips or liquid dye
- Gift tags (optional)

## INSTRUCTIONS

1. Measure the height of the mason jar and divide it evenly into four parts. Use a wax pencil or an easily erasable marker to indicate the divisions (Fig. B). This will help to create even candy cane layers.

2. Place one wick in the bottom of each mason jar. A small square of double-sided adhesive is helpful to secure the wick.

3. Melt 2.6 oz. (75 g) of wax using a water bath and add red candle dye (either dye chips or liquid dye) and mix until evenly incorporated. Note how much dye is used to achieve the desired hue. Once melted, take the wax pot off the heat and allow to cool to 135°F–140°F. Add five drops of peppermint oil or candle scent and stir to incorporate.

4. Pour the red wax to the first mark of each jar. After you have poured the red wax, clean out the wax pot.

5. Melt another 2.6 oz. (75 g) of wax using a water bath. Once melted, take the wax pot off the heat and allow wax to cool to 135°F–140°F. Add five drops of peppermint oil or candle scent.

6. Pour the white wax to the second mark of each jar. Allow to cool for at least an hour.

7. Repeat Steps 3–6 to create the next two stripes.

8. Trim the wick. Allow candle to cool for at least six hours before use.

Yields
2 candles

Fig. A

Fig. B

# COOKIE CUTTER CANDLES

⇢⇢⇢ ◆ ⇠⇠⇠

These make great gifts to bring to holiday parties.
Once the candles burn down, the cookie cutters
can be used to make sweet treats!

## MATERIALS (Fig. A)

- 5 oz. (150 g) soy wax flakes
- (3) 2" (5 cm) mounted cotton wicks
- 3 metal cookie cutters
- Red and green wax color chips or liquid candle dye
- Gaffer tape
- Parchment paper

## INSTRUCTIONS

1. Place your cookie cutters on parchment paper, sharp side down. Using gaffer tape or strong painter's tape, secure the cookie cutters to the paper, creating a seal (Fig. B). Place a small mounted wick in the center of each cookie cutter.

2. Melt 1.75 oz. (50 g) of wax using a water bath. Once melted, take the wax pot off the heat and allow to cool to 135°F–140°F.

3. Slowly pour the wax into one of the cookie cutters (I chose to make the snowflake shape white).

4. Melt another 1.75 oz. (50 g) of wax in a water bath. Add red wax color chips or dye and stir until evenly incorporated.

5. When the wax is between 135°F–140°F, slowly pour into the cookie cutter you wish to be red (I chose the gingerbread man). After you have poured the red wax, clean out the wax pot.

6. Melt the last 1.75 oz. (50 g) of wax in a water bath. Add green wax color chips or dye and stir until evenly incorporated.

7. When the wax is between 135°F–140°F, slowly pour into the cookie cutter you wish to be green (I chose the Christmas tree).

8. Allow candles to cool for two hours and then remove the tape, trim the wicks if needed, and the candles are ready to use or gift!

Fig. A

Fig. B

### Pro Tip

Be sure to place these candles on a plate when you burn them. Wax may leak out of the bottom of the cookie cutter if it burns too long.

# BEESWAX
# FOREST CANDLES

>>>>> ◆ <<<<<

These enchanting evergreens are an easy and fun craft
for kids as they do not involve melting wax.

## MATERIALS (Fig. A)

- Rectangular sheet of beeswax
  (one provided in this kit is 20 x 10 cm)

- (2) 6" (15 cm) woven cotton wicking

- A hairdryer

## INSTRUCTIONS

1. Using a knife or scissors cut the beeswax sheet diagonally from the upper left-hand corner to the bottom right-hand corner of the rectangle, creating two equal triangles.

2. Warm the wax with a hairdryer on the lowest setting to make it more pliable. Don't warm the wax too much; if it turns to liquid, allow it to cool and start again.

3. Place the wick along the tall edge of the triangle and begin to roll the wax over the wick. Continue rolling the wax toward the point of the triangle, keeping the bottom edge in line so the candle will stand up when finished (Fig. A).

4. When you come to the last inch to be rolled, warm it with the hairdryer, then press it firmly to seal it against the candle.

5. Trim the wick if it is over ½" (1 cm) and your rolled tree candle is ready to use!

Fig. A

### Pro Tip

Another kid-friendly project is to create cutouts from the beeswax sheet and use them to decorate pillar candles. Press small cookie cutters into the beeswax sheet to create fun cut-out shapes. Then transform a plain, store-bought pillar candle to a custom centerpiece by applying the beeswax cutouts. Use a hairdryer (on the low setting) to soften the wax, then firmly press the shapes to the pillar candle. Ta-da!

# SPRING
# CANDLES

# LEMON BEESWAX CANDLES

›››››› ♦ ‹‹‹‹‹

Brighten the room with this amazing combination of nature's most soothing scents.

## MATERIALS (Fig. A)

- 3.5 oz. (100 g) of beeswax pastilles
- 4 wooden wicks and mounts
- 2 lemons

## INSTRUCTIONS

1. Cut the lemons lengthwise and carefully peel the fruit from the rind using a knife and citrus spoon. Avoid puncturing or tearing the rind as this will be the vessel for the wax. When you are finished the peel should be free of pulp.

2. Place the wooden wicks in the center of each lemon peel.

3. Melt the beeswax in a water bath. Once melted, take the wax pot off the heat and allow to cool until it is between 140°F–155°F.

4. Pour wax into each of the four lemon halves.

5. Allow to cool fully, between four to six hours. Trim the wicks if needed before lighting.

DIFFICULTY LEVEL ◈◈◈

Yields
4 candles

Fig. A

### Pro Tip

If you want these lemon candles to have that light, fresh lemon look, use them within twenty-four hours of making them. After that the lemon peel will begin to darken and harden (like lemons in potpourri). They still smell great when lit and should not mold since the wax has sealed off all the moisture in the lemon.

# SPRING FLING MASON JAR CANDLES

>>>>> ◆ <<<<<

Pretty as a springtime
garden party.

## MATERIALS (Fig. A)

- 10.5 oz. (300 g) soy wax flakes
- (2) 8 oz. (250 ml) mason jars
- (2) 6" (15 cm) mounted cotton wicks
- 20 drops osmanthus flower candle scent
- 2 tsp (10 g) dried rose petals

DIFFICULTY LEVEL ◆◆◆

Yields
2 candles

## INSTRUCTIONS

1. Place one wick in each mason jar. A small square of double-sided adhesive is helpful to secure the wick to the bottom of the jar.

2. Melt the wax using a water bath. Once melted, take the wax pot off the heat and allow to cool to 135°F–140°F. Add the osmanthus flower candle scent and stir until incorporated, approximately two to three minutes.

3. Slowly pour the wax to the top of each jar. To keep the wick straight, tape it to a pencil or stir stick that rests across the top of the mason jar.

4. Allow to cool for fifteen minutes then drop a few dried rose petals on the top of each jar. If the wax is still too hot and the petals sink, wait another ten minutes then try again. The goal is to have the rose petals embed in the still-warm top of the candle.

5. Allow to cool thoroughly for six to eight hours then trim the wick so it is ½" (1 cm).

6. Decorate the jars as you wish with ribbons and flowers.

Fig. A

### Aromatherapy Candles

Have you ever been told to stop and smell the roses? Well, according to aromatherapy, that's good advice! Aromatherapy believes that many natural scents can promote health and well-being for your mind, body, and soul. Osmanthus flower, the scent that is included with this kit, is popular among perfumers as it is believed to create feelings of happiness when inhaled. It is also invigorating and thought to relieve fatigue, making it the perfect scent for this spring candle.

# LOTS OF LOVE CANDLES

⟫⟫⟫⟫ ◆ ⟪⟪⟪⟪

Is romance in the air?
Set the mood with these sweetheart candles.

## MATERIALS (Fig. A)

- 7 oz. (200 g) soy wax flakes
- 16 oz. (0.5 L) empty milk carton
- Heart-shaped candy mold
- 6" (15 cm) mounted wick
- Red wax color chips or liquid dye

## INSTRUCTIONS

1. Cut the top off the milk carton and place a wick in the center by taping it to the bottom.

2. Melt 3.5 oz. (100 g) of wax using a water bath. Stir in the red wax dye and mix until incorporated. Once melted and the color is incorporated, take the wax pot off the heat and allow to cool to 135°F–140°F.

3. Pour the red wax into the heart-shaped candy mold. You will need to make approximately fifteen to twenty hearts. After you have poured the red wax, clean out the wax pot. To do so, use a paper towel to wipe out the inside of the wax pot while the remaining wax is still liquid. Allow the wax hearts to cool for one to two hours, depending on the size of the heart molds.

4. Once cooled, pop the hearts out of the mold and set aside.

5. Heat the remaining 3.5 oz. (100 g) of wax using a water bath. Once melted, take the wax pot off the heat and allow to cool to 135°F–140°F.

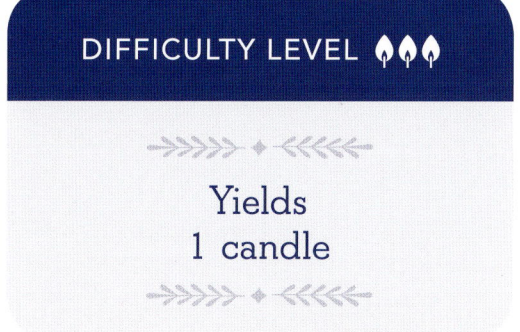

DIFFICULTY LEVEL ◆◆◆

Yields
1 candle

Fig. A

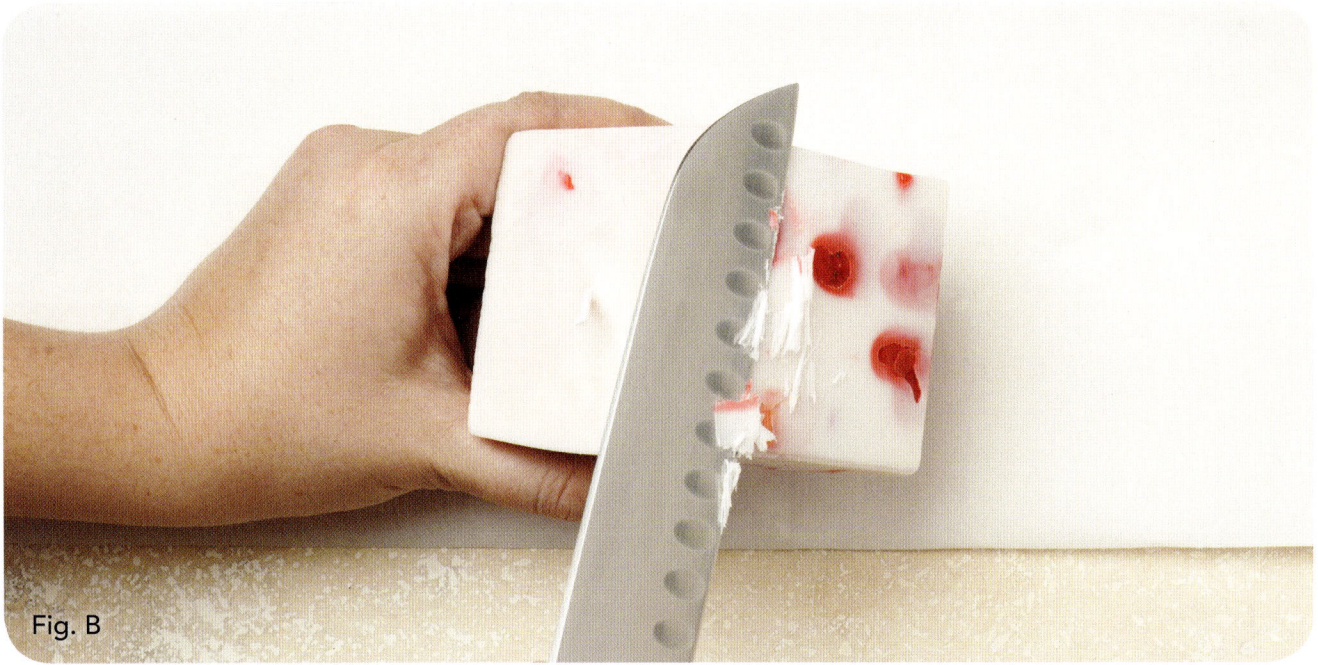

Fig. B

6. While the wax cools to the proper temperature, stack the wax hearts around the inside edges of the milk carton. If you are having trouble getting the hearts to stay in place, dip a paintbrush (a cheap or old one you are okay dedicating to wax!) into the melted white wax and dab molten wax onto the front of the wax hearts. Then quickly stick them to the side of the milk carton. Hold them in place for a few seconds and they should adhere.

7. Pour the white wax into the milk carton after you have arranged the hearts. If the wick wobbles, keep it in place by taping it to a pencil that rests across the milk carton. Allow wax to cool for three to four hours.

8. After the wax has cooled, peel away the milk carton and trim the wick.

9. With a sharp knife gently carve the sides of the candle until the red hearts become clear (Fig. B). Continue to carve away the sides of the candle until the red embedded hearts are visible.

## Pro Tip

I borrowed this idea of adding the embedded hearts from crafty soapmakers. Play around with other shapes and motifs; yellow stars in a dark blue candle for example.

## Candle Color

I have found that candle color chips are more potent than the liquid dye. However, in both cases, a little dye goes a long way, so it is best to start by adding a small amount and gradually build up to the color you desire. The wax color will also change once it has cooled. To test it, drip some wax onto parchment paper to judge the color and adjust accordingly. If you find that the color is too dark, add more wax chips.

# SUMMER
# CANDLES

# SUMMER NIGHTS FLOATING CANDLES

>>>>> ◆ <<<<<

Dress up any backyard barbecue
on those warm summer nights.

## MATERIALS

- 3.5 oz. (100 g) soy wax flakes
- Star and heart floating candle molds
- Neon pink wax dye flakes or liquid dye
- Bright yellow wax dye flakes or liquid dye
- (2) 2" (5 cm) mounted wicks

## INSTRUCTIONS

1. Wipe the star and heart candle molds with cooking oil and place a mounted wick in the center of each star and heart mold.

2. Melt 1.75 oz. (50 g) of wax in the wax pot using a water bath. Once melted, take the wax pot off the heat and allow to cool to 135°F–140°F.

3. Stir in the neon pink wax dye into the melted wax and mix until incorporated.

4. Pour the pink wax into the heart-shaped molds. After pouring, clean out the wax pot.

5. Melt the remaining 1.75 oz. (50 g) of wax in the wax pot using a water bath. When it is the correct temperature, add the bright yellow wax dye and stir until incorporated.

6. Pour the yellow wax into the star-shaped molds. After pouring, clean out the wax pot.

7. Allow the candles to cool in their molds for one to two hours.

8. Once hardened, pop them out of their molds, trim their wicks, and set them afloat! (Fig. A)

**DIFFICULTY LEVEL** ◆◆◆

⇢⇢⇢ ✦ ⇠⇠⇠
### Yields
### 2 candles
⇢⇢⇢ ✦ ⇠⇠⇠

**Fig. A**

### Pro Tip

Have some extra wax from a previous project? The shallow floating candle mold does not require much wax and making a floating candle or two on the side is a great way to use up any excess wax. Then you'll be party-ready any time!

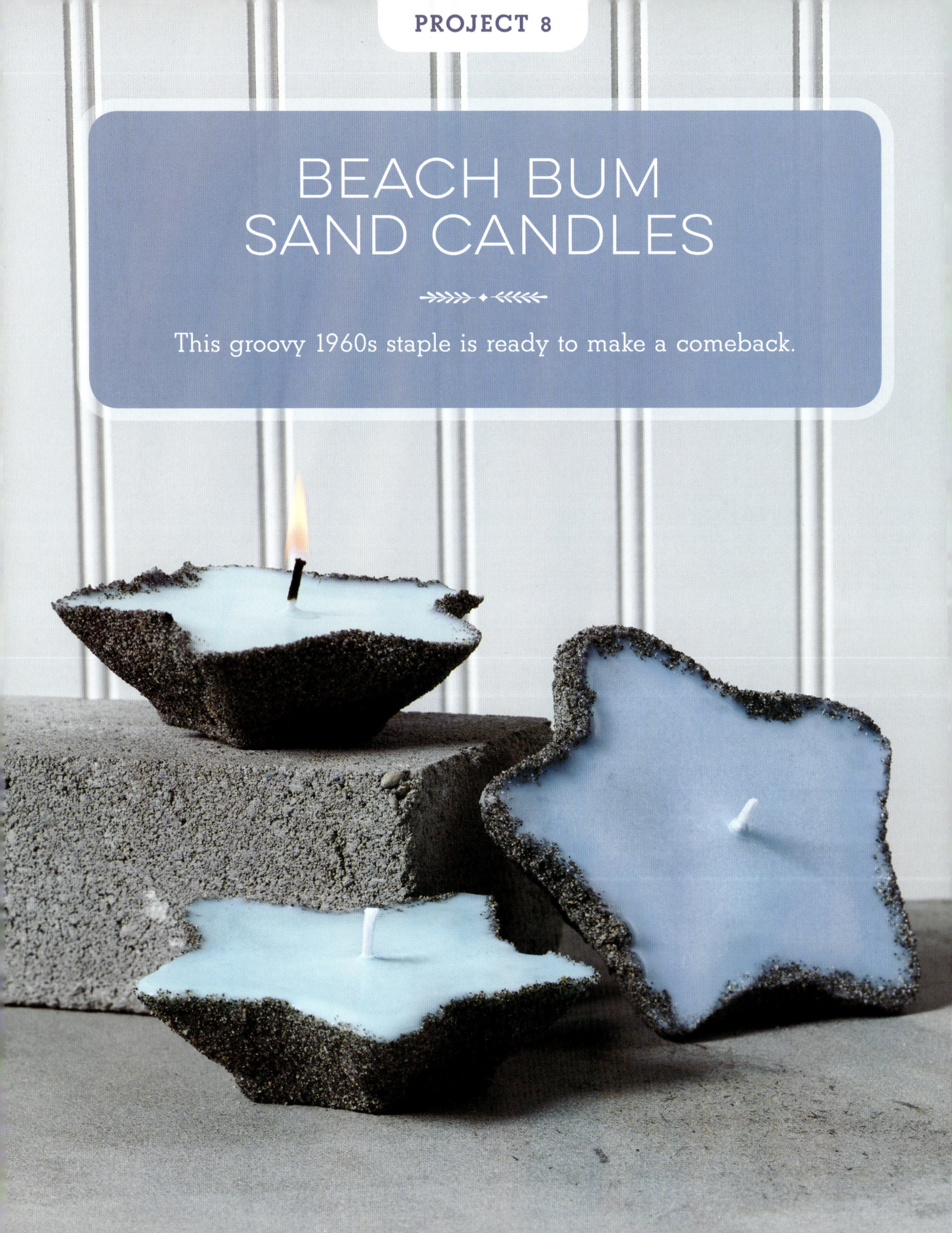

# BEACH BUM SAND CANDLES

>>>>> ✦ <<<<<

This groovy 1960s staple is ready to make a comeback.

## MATERIALS (Fig. A)

- 7 oz. (200 g) soy wax flakes
- Small bowl or container
- Teal wax dye flakes or liquid dye
- Sand (in a large bowl)
- (2) 2" (5 cm) mounted wicks

## INSTRUCTIONS

1. Make sure the sand in your bowl is damp enough to hold the shape of any impression made into it. Spray the sand with water if it is too dry. Be sure there isn't any standing water in the sand.

2. Press your small bowl (here I use a small star-shaped condiment bowl) into the sand and carefully remove it leaving its impression. Do this twice. Place a mounted wick in the center of each impression.

3. Melt the wax in the wax pot using a water bath. Once melted, take the wax pot off the heat and allow to cool to 135°F–140°F.

4. Stir in the teal wax dye into the melted wax and mix until incorporated.

5. Pour the wax into the sand impressions (Fig B).

6. Allow to cool for two to three hours then remove them from the sand. Shake off any excess sand and trim the wicks.

Fig. A

Fig. B

# MODERN PILLAR CANDLES

⋙⋙⋙ ◆ ⋘⋘⋘

These minimalist beauties
will steal the show.

## MATERIALS (Fig. A)

- 7 oz. (200 g) soy wax flakes
- Plastic water bottle
- 1 lb. (0.45 kg) plaster powder
- Black acrylic paint
- Cooking spray
- Water
- Box cutter
- Large Bowl

### DIFFICULTY LEVEL ♦♦♦

Yields
1 candle

Fig. A

## INSTRUCTIONS

1. With the box cutter, cut off the top of the water bottle. Coat the inside of the water bottle with cooking spray or vegetable oil. Set aside.

2. In a large bowl, mix the plaster by following the directions on the packaging; each brand may vary. While mixing it, add black paint until you get the shade of gray you desire. Note: you may use cement instead of plaster, in which case you won't need to add black paint as it is naturally gray.

3. Pour the plaster into the water bottle until it is approximately 3–4" (7–10 cm) high. Tap the bottle against your work surface a couple times to help settle the plaster and get any air bubbles out. If you wish to angle your plaster layer, prop the water bottle on its side. Make sure it is secure and will stay in place.

### Pro Tip

Another benefit of using plaster over real cement in this project is that white plaster can absorb any color paint so you are not limited to making the base look concrete grey. Try a calming dark purple, spirited matcha green or coordinate with your home decor.

Fig. B

4. Let dry for twenty-four hours then place a long mounted wick in the center of the bottle.

5. Melt the wax in the wax pot using a water bath. Once melted, take the wax pot off the heat and allow to cool to 135°F–140°F.

6. Pour the wax on top of the plaster layer (Fig. B). Keep the wick in place by taping or wrapping it around a pencil until the wax has hardened.

7. Allow to dry for four to six hours.

8. Once dry, use the box cutter to slowly and carefully make two cuts down the length of the water bottle, approximately 2" (5 cm) apart to create a freed section. You need to cut through the plastic while not damaging the candle. Pull down the freed piece of bottle then pry the candle free.

9. Trim the wick, place it on a tray or plate, and you are ready to light it.

## Housewarming Tradition

A candle makes a great housewarming gift. Since medieval times, it is believed that lighting a candle on the first night in a new home can bestow blessings, ward off evil spirits, and symbolically cast out darkness.

## Pro Tip

Finding the right plastic container is key! If the container is too stiff, it makes removing the candle very difficult and you may damage it. I recommend test squeezing all the water bottles at the grocery store (you might get stares from other shoppers) to find the thinnest and most flexible. For shorter versions of this candle, large yogurt containers work well.

---

# FALL
# CANDLES

# TEA FOR TWO CANDLES

⤞⤞⤞ ◆ ⤝⤝⤝

These beauties make wonderful bridal shower or tea party gifts,
and the bergamot gives them a divine Earl Grey aroma.

## MATERIALS (Fig. A)

- 7 oz. (200 g) soy wax flakes
- 1 teacup
- 6" (15 cm) mounted cotton wick
- Bergamot oil
- Loose leaf tea

## INSTRUCTIONS

1. Clean the teacup and place the wick in the bottom of it. A piece of double-sided tape can help hold the wick in place.

2. Melt the wax in the wax pot using a water bath. Once melted, take the wax pot off the heat and allow to cool to 135°F–140°F. Add five to ten drops of bergamot oil and stir to incorporate.

3. Pour the wax into the teacup until it is almost to the top.

4. Allow to cool for fifteen minutes and add a pinch of loose leaf tea on the top. If the wax is still too hot and the tea sinks, wait another ten minutes then try again. The goal is to have the tea embed in the still-warm top of the candle.

5. Let the candle cool three to four hours then trim the wick, and it is ready to use.

**DIFFICULTY LEVEL** ♦♦♦

Yields
1 candle

Fig. A

### Pro Tip

Keep an eye out for inexpensive teacups at thrift stores, estate sales, or whenever you run across a wealthy dowager cleaning house.

# COFFEE DATE CANDLES

⤳⟫⟫⟫ ◆ ⟪⟪⟪⤸

The coffee beans in this candle aren't just for show; they will fill the room with their inviting aroma as the candle burns.

## MATERIALS (Fig. A)

- 8.8 oz. (250 g) soy wax flakes
- 1 stemless wine glass
- 6" (15 cm) mounted cotton wick
- 2 tbsp (27 g) coffee beans
- Brown wax color chips or liquid dye

## INSTRUCTIONS

1. Place the wick in the bottom of the glass. A piece of double-sided tape can help hold the wick in place.

2. Melt 3.5 oz. (100 g) of wax using a water bath. Once melted, take the wax pot off the heat and allow to cool to 135°F–140°F. Stir in the brown wax dye until a dark brown color is achieved.

3. Pour ⅔ of the dark brown wax into the bottom third of the glass leaving ⅓ of the wax in the wax pot.

4. While the dark brown wax cools in the glass, add another 3.5 oz. (100 g) wax to the wax pot and melt it, stirring occasionally. This batch of wax will be a lighter brown color.

5. Allow to cool until it is between 135°F–140°F then pour into the glass until it is ¾ full. Sprinkle a tablespoon of coffee beans into the glass; it is all right if they sink into the wax.

6. Immediately after you have poured the second layer of brown wax, clean out the wax pot.

7. In the clean wax pot, melt the last 1.75 oz. (50 g) of wax. Once it is the correct temperature, pour it into the glass.

8. Allow to cool for fifteen minutes and drop a few coffee beans on the top. If the wax is still too hot and the beans sink into the wax, wait another ten minutes then try again. The goal is to have the coffee beans embed in the still-warm top of the candle.

9. Let the candle cool three to four hours then trim the wick, and it is ready to use.

Fig. A

# APPLE CINNAMON VOTIVE CANDLES

>>>> ◆ <<<<

Warm up your holidays with the cozy
aroma of apples and cinnamon.

## MATERIALS (Fig. A)

- 5 oz. (150 g) soy wax flakes
- 8 oz. (236 ml) paper cup
- 6" (15 cm) mounted cotton wick
- 10–12 cinnamon sticks
- Red wax color chips or liquid dye

## INSTRUCTIONS

1. Melt all the wax in the wax pot using a water bath. Once melted, take the wax pot off the heat and allow to cool to 135°F–140°F.

2. Stir the red wax dye into the melted wax and mix until incorporated.

3. While you are waiting for the wax to cool to pouring temperature, dip the bottoms of the cinnamon sticks into the melted wax, then stick them to the inside of the paper cup (Fig. B). Repeat this until the inside of the cup is lined with cinnamon sticks.

4. Add a wick to the center of the cup.

5. Pour the red wax into the cup. If the wick wobbles, keep it in place by taping it to a pencil that rests across the cup.

6. Allow to cool four to six hours then peel away the paper cup and trim the wick.

7. Decorate the sides of the votive as you wish, and make sure to place a plate under it when you burn it to collect any dripping wax.

Yields
1 candle

Fig. A

Fig. B

# ABOUT THE AUTHOR

Meredith Mennitt is a craft connoisseur and weekend artist. After living in a tiny studio apartment in New York City for over a decade, she is an expert at making big, crafty messes in small spaces. She often has multiple projects going at once, rotating between painting, writing, stitching, and any other craft that crosses her path (except knitting. Team Crochet all the way.) Meredith currently lives in Seattle with her dachshund, Watson.

# MORE CANDLE SAFETY TIPS

Trim candlewicks to ¼ inch (6mm) each time before burning. Keeping your wick short will prevent your candle from burning unevenly.

If there is a carbon buildup "cap" on your wick, cut it off to avoid the flame getting too large .

Don't burn candles for more than 4 hours and don't leave burning candles unattended.

Avoid moving candles once they are lit.

Place candles at least 4 inches (10 cm) apart from one another.

The best way to extinguish a candle is with a candle snuffer. They're fun to use and unlike blowing out candles, snuffers prevent hot wax from splattering.

Keep foreign materials away from lit wick.

If your candle is in glass jar, keep your wick short and centered in the jar so the flame is never in contact with the edge of the jar as that could crack the glass.

Extinguish candles when only ¼ inch of wax remains.